SECLUDED

CHELLEY

To be secluded isn't always a bad thing. Solitude can be rewarding for us and necessary to grow. Let go of all your problems and come out full.

Secluded (adjective)

Not seen or visited by many people; sheltered and private.

For your day to be productive you must...

What are you thankful for?

Weak people seek
revenge.

Strong people
forgive.

Intelligent people
ignore.

How was your day? Let it out.

"Here's what I want you to do:
Find a quiet, secluded place so you
won't be tempted to role-play before
God. Just be there as simply and
honestly as you can manage. The focus
will shift from you to God, and you will
begin to sense his grace."

Matthew 6:6

Your playlist right now?

"The Lord will fight for you; you need only to be still"...Exodus 14:14

Name the ways you were blessed today...

Follow your
Heart but take your
Brain with
you.

How was your day?

What holds you back?

"The Lord is good to those whose hope is in him, to the one who seeks him; it is good to wait quietly for the salvation of the Lord. It is good for man to bear the yoke while he is young. Let him sit alone in silence, for the Lord has laid it on him."

Lamentations 3:25-28

What do you love about yourself?

Lighten up, just enjoy life,
smile more, laugh more,
and don't get so worked
up about things.

Kenneth Branagh

Strengths?

My mission in life is
not merely to
survive, but to
thrive.

Maya Angelou

Weakness?

Protect your peace

always and stay true

to your vision.

How was your day?

Keep pushing.
Don't let a setback
create your
breakdown, let it
create your
breakthrough.

How was your day?

Be still, and know
that I am God; I
will be exalted
among the nations,
I will be exalted in
the earth."

Psalm 46:10

What are your priorities in life?

Every thought

creates your future.

How was your day?

If there is no struggle, there is no progress.

Frederick Douglas

How was your day?

In life journey

always keep the

faith.

How was your day?

The Lord is my shepherd, I shall not want.

Psalms 23:1

How was your day?

Hope this Journal has helped you to

release some of your inner thoughts

and concerns you may have on your

life journey.

Xoxo, Chelley